Math in Focus®

Singapore Math®
by Marshall Cavendish

Extra Practice and Homework

Program Consultant
Dr. Fong Ho Kheong

Author
Dr. Ng Wee Leng

Marshall Cavendish
Education

U.S. Distributor

Houghton Mifflin Harcourt.
The Learning Company™

Course 1B

© 2020 Marshall Cavendish Education Pte Ltd

Published by Marshall Cavendish Education
Times Centre, 1 New Industrial Road, Singapore 536196
Customer Service Hotline: (65) 6213 9688
US Office Tel: (1-914) 332 8888 | Fax: (1-914) 332 8882
E-mail: cs@mceducation.com
Website: www.mceducation.com

Distributed by
Houghton Mifflin Harcourt
125 High Street
Boston, MA 02110
Tel: 617-351-5000
Website: www.hmhco.com/programs/math-in-focus

First published 2020

ISBN 978-0-358-10309-7

Printed in Singapore

5 6 7 8 9 10   1401   26 25 24 23 22
4500840211   B C D E F

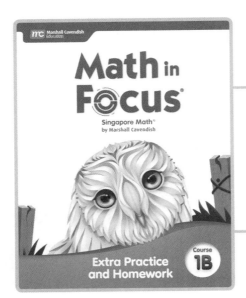

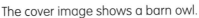

The cover image shows a barn owl.
Owls live in trees or sometimes in the top of barns. They are mostly nocturnal, so they usually come out at night. They have large eyes that are fixed in place, so they rely on their ability to turn their necks 270° to scan their surroundings. Their ears are asymmetrically shaped and positioned, allowing their brains to calculate the exact location of their prey in total darkness. They are excellent hunters who eat mostly rodents.

Contents

© 2020 Marshall Cavendish Education Pte Ltd

Preface

Welcome!

Math in F☺cus®: *Extra Practice and Homework* is written to complement the Student Edition in your learning journey.

The book provides carefully constructed activities and problems that parallel what you have learned in the Student Edition.

- **Activities** are designed to help you achieve proficiency in the math concepts and to develop confidence in your mathematical abilities.

- **MATH JOURNAL** is included to provide you with opportunities to reflect on the learning in the chapter.

- **PUT ON YOUR THINKING CAP!** allows you to improve your critical thinking and problem-solving skills, as well as to be challenged as you solve problems in novel ways.

You may use a calculator whenever  appears.

BLANK

Chapter 7

Extra Practice and Homework
Algebraic Expressions

Activity 1   Use Letters to Represent Numbers

Write an algebraic expression for each statement.

1 Sum of *h* and 4

2 *x* more than 12

3 Product of *k* and 5

4 Quotient of *p* and 3

5 Subtract 8 from *d*

6 6 less than *b*

7 7 groups of *c*

8 Divide *y* by 9

9 Nellie has *q* stickers.

  a Jane has 9 fewer stickers than Nellie. How many stickers does Jane have in terms of *q*?

  b Jacob has 4 times as many stickers as Nellie. How many stickers does Jacob have in terms of *q*?

  c Fred has 23 more stickers than Nellie. How many stickers does Fred have in terms of *q*?

  d Karen has $\frac{3}{7}$ as many stickers as Nellie. How many stickers does Karen have in terms of *q*?

10 Add 15 to the product of y and 3.

11 Divide m by 5, and then subtract 12 from the quotient.

12 Multiply b by 3, then divide the product by 8.

13 The price of a sling bag, given that it costs twice as much as a box of cards that costs m dollars.

14 The total number of seashells Mandy and Ken have, given that Mandy has $4s$ seashells and Ken has 12 more seashells than Mandy.

Solve.

15 In a bakery, a bag of croissants costs y dollars. A loaf of multi-grain bread costs $3 more than a bag of croissants. Mr. Potter pays $45 for some loaves of multi-grain bread. Write the number of loaves of bread he buys in terms of y.

16 Ben has some goldfish in a fish tank. The ratio of orange goldfish to yellow goldfish is 3 : 5. He has $6f$ orange goldfish. Write the number of yellow goldfish he has in terms of f.

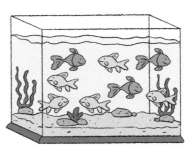

Activity 2 Evaluating Algebraic Expressions

Evaluate each expression for the given value of the variable.

1 $3a + 4$ when $a = 6$

2 $9b - 8$ when $b = 3$

3 $22c - 8$ when $c = 2$

4 $35 - 7d$ when $d = 5$

5 $20 + \frac{7}{8}e$ when $e = 16$

6 $\frac{3}{4}f - 2$ when $f = 8$

Solve.

7 There are x colored pencils in a box. Write an expression in terms of x for each statement and evaluate the expression when $x = 24$.

  a The number of colored pencils in 3 boxes.

  b The number of colored pencils each child gets when a box of coloured pencils and 6 colored pencils are shared equally among 5 children.

8 Kaitlyn drinks y pints of milk every day. Write an expression in terms of y for each statement and evaluate the expression when $y = \frac{1}{2}$.

  a The total amount of milk drank in 5 days in pints.

  b The amount of milk left, in pints, if Kaitlyn drank from a 1 gallon full milk bottle.

Evaluate each expression when $r = 8$.

9 $5(10r - 3) + (6r - 1)$

10 $6(4r + 3) - 2(5r - 8)$

11 $5(2r + 5) + \dfrac{3r - 3}{4}$

12 $\dfrac{5r + 6}{6} + \dfrac{3r - 2}{4} + \dfrac{3r}{2}$

Evaluate each of the following when $k = 5$.

13 Subtract 40 from the sum of $8k$ and 12

14 Product of $(3k + 1)$ and $(3k - 5)$

15 Sum of $\dfrac{5(k + 3)}{6}$ and $\dfrac{2(k - 1)}{3}$

16 Divide $4(k - 1)$ by $(k + 5)$

Chapter

7

Extra Practice and Homework
Algebraic Expressions

Activity 3   Simplifying Algebraic Expressions

Simplify each expression. Then, state the coefficient of the variable in each expression.

1 $a + a - 5 + 7$

2 $b + b - b - 7 + 4$

Simplify each expression.

3 $5c + 4c - 7c + c$

4 $12d - 5d + 8d + 9d$

5 $8e - 3e + 5e + 8e$

6 $15f + 4f - 5f - 2f$

7 $9p + 13 - 8p + 7 - 5p$

8 $16 + 12q - 9 + 7q - 4q + 11$

9 $24 + 3r + 5r - 13 + 4r - 13r$

10 $21s - 19 + 2s - 24s + 15 - 7s$

State whether each pair of expressions is equivalent.

11 $2g + 5g$ and $4g + 5g - 2g$

12 $7h$ and $7 + h$

13 $3j + 2$ and $2 - 3j$

14 $4k + 3k$ and $\frac{18k}{6} + 2k$

Solve.

15 Kelly cycles from her home to school. She cycles $2a$ miles south, $(5a - 9)$ miles east, and $(5a + 6)$ miles south to reach her school. How far does Kelly cycle?

16 Lucas had 20b liters of milk. He drank 3b liters of milk every day. How much milk was left after 4 days?

17 The cost of a doll is 7x dollars and the cost of a key chain is x dollars. Find the total cost of the 3 dolls and 4 key chains in terms of x.

18. Mrs. Lee works $4y$ hours each day from Monday to Friday. She works $(4y - 4)$ hours on Saturday. Mrs. Lee does not work on Sunday. Find the number of hours Mrs. Lee works in one week in terms of y.

19. Mr. Mason shared a taxi with his friends. They evenly shared the fare of $56 among the z of them. Mr. Mason also gave a $10 tip. Find the amount of money Mr. Mason paid in terms of z.

Chapter 7

Extra Practice and Homework
Algebraic Expressions

Activity 4   Expanding and Factoring Algebraic Expressions

Expand each expression.

1 $4(3a + 7)$

2 $5(3 - 6b)$

3 $2(4c + 9)$

4 $7(2d - 5)$

Factor each expression.

5 $5e + 15$

6 $9 - 18f$

7 $21 + 18g$

8 $30h + 15$

State whether each pair of expressions is equivalent.

9 $5(2j - 3)$ and $10j + 15$

10 $10(3 + 4k)$ and $40k + 30$

11 $4(3m - 5)$ and $12m - 20$

12 $3(n + 3)$ and $9n + 9$

Expand and simplify each expression.

13 $8(4p - 3) + 5(7 + 10p)$

14 $11(4 + 5q) - 14q - 8$

15 $7(5 + 4r) + 9(2 - r)$

16 $3(8s - 5) + 4s - 2$

Simplify each expression. Then, factor the expression.

17 $14 - 29t + 5(7 + 10t)$

18 $3(4 + 5u) + 6(3u + 8)$

19 $4v - 12 + 9(3 - v)$

20 $4(2w + 5) + 4(3w - 2)$

Solve.

21 A train is moving at an average speed of $(4a + 7)$ miles per hour. Write an expression in terms of a for the distance traveled by the train in 4 hours.

4 Expanding and Factoring Algebraic Expressions

22 A pound of ham costs $(3b + 5)$ dollars and a pound of beef costs $(6b + 7)$ dollars. Mrs. Smith bought 3 pounds of ham and 2 pounds of beef. Write an expression in terms of b for the amount Mrs. Smith paid for the two items.

23 The average height of 5 children is $(9c + 4)$ centimeters. Two more children with heights of $(10c + 7)$ centimeters and $(14c - 3)$ centimeters join the group. Find the average height of the 7 children in terms of c.

Chapter 7
Extra Practice and Homework
Algebraic Expressions

Activity 5 Real-World Problems: Algebraic Expressions

Solve.

1 Steven had $250. He bought some T-shirts at $8 each and had $q left. How many T-shirts did he buy?

You can use the four-step problem-solving model to help you.

2 Sara and Sofia took part in a relay race. Sara took 25 minutes to finish her section and Sofia took y minutes longer to complete hers. What was the total time they took to complete the race in terms of y?

3 Amanda, Bruno and Carla collected bottle caps for charity. Amanda collected $(4f - 3)$ bottle caps. Bruno collects twice as many bottle caps as Amanda. Carla collects $3(5 + 2f)$ bottles. How many bottles did they collect altogether in terms of f?

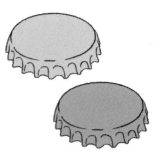

4 Alex's house is located c miles from his school. The shopping mall is 4 miles farther from his house to his school. The library is 2 miles less than twice the distance from his house to his school.

a Write an expression that shows the distance from Alex's house to the shopping mall.

b Write an expression that shows the distance from Alex's house to the library.

c If $c = 4$, is the shopping mall or the library closer to his house? How much closer?

5 Carla can make 5*d* doll dresses in 3 hours.

    a Write an expression that shows the number of doll dresses Carla can make in 7 hours in terms of *d*.

    b If *d* = 6, how many doll dresses can Carla make in 7 hours?

6 The total price of a sandwich and a drink is $8. The price of the sandwich is $*p*.

    a Express the price of the drink in terms of *p*.

    b If the price of the sandwich is $4.20, find the price of the drink.

7 Jade is w years old now.

    a Find her age 8 years ago.

    b Jade's mother is 5 years older than 3 times Jade's age now. Express her mother's age in terms of w.

8 In an examination, Ronnie scores $4x$ marks for Mathematics, $(3x + 5)$ marks for English and $(5x + 7)$ marks for Science.

    a Find and simplify an expression in x, for her total mark for the three subjects.

    b If $x = 15$, find her total mark for the three subjects.

Name: _____ Date: _____

Mathematical Habit 7 Make use of structure

Meili made a list of equivalent expressions for $3x - 2$.

$x + x + x - 1 - 1$	$2x + x - 1 + 3$	$2(2x + 1) - 4$
$3 + x - 2$	$\frac{5x}{3} + \frac{4x}{3} - \frac{5}{2} + \frac{1}{2}$	$x + x + x - 2$
$3x - 1 - 1$	$2(x - 1) + x$	$4x + x + 3 - 5$

a Hiro said there are some wrong expressions. Do you agree? If so, state those wrong expressions.

b Give three more examples of equivalent expressions for $3x - 2$. Explain your answers.

Mathematical Habit **1** Persevere in solving problems

The diagram shows two different rectangles, *A* and *B*. The perimeters of the rectangles are the same.

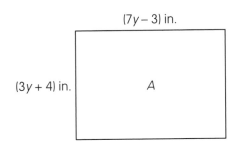

(7y – 3) in.

(3y + 4) in.

A

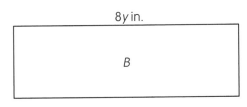

8y in.

B

a Find the width of rectangle *B* in terms of *y*.

b If *y* = 3 inches, find the sum of the perimeters of the rectangles.

Chapter 8

Extra Practice and Homework
Equations and Inequalities

Activity 1   Solving Algebraic Equations

Solve each equation using the substitution method.

1 $5 + a = 20$

2 $7 - b = 5$

3 $9c = 81$

4 $\dfrac{d}{2} = 6$

Solve each equation using the concept of balancing.

5 $f + 14 = 20$

6 $12 - g = 3$

7 $3h = 12$

8 $\dfrac{j}{3} = 9$

Solve each equation using the concept of balancing. Express each answer in its simplest form.

9 $k + \frac{1}{3} = 2$

10 $\frac{5}{6} + \ell = \frac{7}{6}$

11 $m - \frac{1}{3} = \frac{4}{3}$

12 $\frac{3}{4}n = 6$

13 $2p = \frac{1}{3}$

14 $\frac{2}{5}q = \frac{3}{10}$

15 $r + 1.4 = 4.6$

16 $4.2 + s = 7.8$

17 $t - 2.8 = 5.7$

18 $34.9 - v = 20.1$

19 $3.4w = 51$

20 $2.5z = 25$

Solve.

21 Choose two numbers from the box, such that when they are inserted into the equation below, the solution of the equation is 6.

$$x - \boxed{?} = \boxed{?}$$

5		8		2
	3		1	

Look for the two numbers that have a difference of 6.

22 Choose two numbers from the box, such that when they are inserted into the equation below, the solution of the equation is $2\frac{1}{3}$.

$$\boxed{?} \, x = \boxed{?}$$

1		3		2
	7		5	

Rewrite $2\frac{1}{3}$ into an improper fraction.

Chapter 8

Extra Practice and Homework
Equations and Inequalities

Activity 2   Writing Linear Equations

Solve.

1. Alan has x sunflowers. Bella has 3 times as many sunflowers as Alan.

    a If y stands for the number of sunflowers Bella has, express y in terms of x.

    b State the independent and dependent variables in the equation.

2. Mrs. Kim buys $2x$ pounds of ham. Mrs. Lee buys 2.5 pounds less than Mrs. Kim.

    a If the amount Mrs. Lee buys is y pounds of ham, express y in terms of x.

    b State the independent and dependent variables in the equation.

3. Pedro has 6 liters of orange juice. He drinks n liters each day.

    a If Pedro has m liters of orange juice left after one week, express m in terms of n.

    b State the independent and dependent variables in the equation.

4. Rachel saved q dollars. Sofia saved $\frac{1}{4}$ of the amount that Rachel saved.

   a. If p represents the amount Sofia saved, express p in terms of q.

   b. State the independent and dependent variables in the equation.

5. The initial temperature of a glass of melting ice was 0 degree Celsius. The temperature of the melting ice increased by 2 degrees Celsius every minute. After x minutes, the temperature of the glass of melting ice is y degree Celsius.

   a. Write an equation relating x and y.

   b. Fill in the table to show the relationship between x and y.

Time (x min)	0	1	2	3	4
Temperature (y °C)	0				

6. At a supermarket, tomatoes are sold at $2.50 per pound. The cost of x pounds of tomatoes sold is y dollars.

   a. Write an equation relating x and y.

   b. Fill in the table to show the relationship between x and y.

Weight of Tomatoes (x lb)	1	2	3	4	5
Cost of Tomatoes ($$y$)	2.5				

7 A car weighs 2,450 pounds when there are no fuel in the tank. For every 1 gallon of fuel added, the car weighs 5 pounds heavier. The weight of the car is y pounds when there are x gallons of fuel in the tank.

a Express y in terms of x.

b Make a table to show the relationship between y and x. Use values of $x = 10, 20, 30, 40,$ and 50 in your table.

c Graph the relationship between y and x on a coordinate plane.

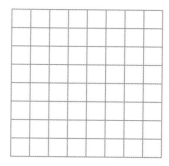

8 A factory water tank has 880 gallons of water. It bursts and loses water at a rate of 20 gallons per minute. After *x* minutes, there are *y* gallons of water left in the tank.

a Express *y* in terms of *x*.

b Make a table to show the relationship between *y* and *x*. Use values of *x* = 0, 1, 2, 3, and 4 in your table.

c Graph the relationship between *y* and *x* on a coordinate plane.

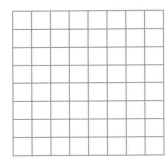

d Use your graph to find the volume of water left in the tank after 2 minutes.

9 The rental charge for a badminton court is \$18 for 2 hours. The charge for renting the court for x hours is y dollars.

a Express y in terms of x.

b Make a table to show the relationship between y and x. Use values of $x = 0$, 1, 2, 3, and 4 in your table.

c Graph the relationship between y and x on a coordinate plane.

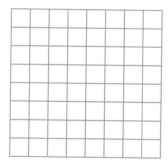

2 Writing Linear Equations

10 Claire walked 1.5 miles at a constant speed for 30 minutes. She walked y miles after x minutes.

   a Express y in terms of x.

   b Make a table to show the relationship between y and x. Use values of $x = 10, 20, 30, 40,$ and 50 in your table.

   c Graph the relationship between y and x on a coordinate plane.

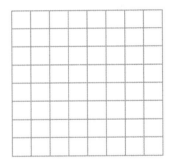

   d Use your graph to find the distance she walked after 45 minutes.

Chapter 8 Extra Practice and Homework
Equations and Inequalities

Activity 3 Real-World Problems: Equations

Write an algebraic equation for each problem. Then, solve.

1 When 93 is subtracted from a number, the result is 129. What is the number?

Use algebra to represent an unknown number or value.

2 The length of a rectangle is 2 inches longer than its width. The perimeter is 40 inches. Find its width.

Perimeter = 40 in.

3　When a number is halved, the result is 29. What is the number?

4　Daniel spends the same amount of money every day. He spends $48 in 12 days. How much does he spend each day?

5 The height of a growing plant seedling is 6 centimeters. It grows to a new height of 9.6 centimeters the next day. Find the percent of increase in height.

6 Some participants were invited to an event but only $\frac{5}{7}$ of them attended. 45 participants attended the event. Find the number of participants who are invited to the event.

7 The number of books Paige reads to the number of books Autumn reads every month is 5 : 4. Autumn read 24 books this month. How many books did Paige read this month?

8 The membership of a gym comprises a one-time sign-up fee that costs $78 and a monthly fee of $25. How many months will a member have used the gym if he pays an amount of $228?

Chapter 8 — Extra Practice and Homework
Equations and Inequalities

Activity 4   Solutions of Simple Inequalities

Rewrite each statement using >, <, ≥, or ≤.

1 *a* is less than or equal to 65.

2 *b* is greater than or equal to 37.

3 *c* is greater than 23.

4 *d* is less than 13.

5 The mass of a piece of luggage on flight is at most 30 kilograms. Write an inequality to represent the mass of the piece of luggage.

Represent the solution set of each inequality on a number line.

6 $e > 9$

7 $f < 7$

8 $g \geq 12$

9 $h \leq 11$

Match each inequality to its graph.

   a $x \leq 8$ **b** $x > 3$ **c** $x < 7$ **d** $x \geq 6$

10
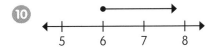

11
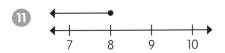

12

13
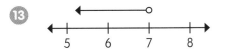

Write an inequality for each number line.

14

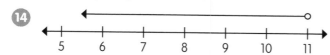

15

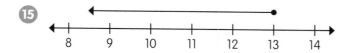

16

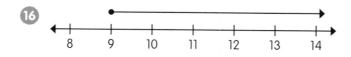

17

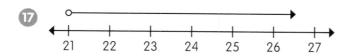

Represent the solution set of each inequality on a number line and give three possible solutions of each inequality.

18 $b \leq 11.3$

19 $c \geq 3\frac{1}{3}$

20 $d < 2.5$

21 $f \leq 9\frac{2}{5}$

22 $g > \frac{56}{9}$

23 $h \geq 6.24$

24 $j < \frac{35}{4}$

25 $k > 5.35$

Solve.

26 In the inequality $x > 7.4$, x represents the distance of Layla's school from her house in miles.

    a Is 9 a possible value of x? Explain.

    b Is $7\frac{2}{3}$ a possible value of x? Explain.

    c Draw a number line to represent the solution set of the inequality. State the least possible distance of Layla's school from her house, as an integer.

27 In the inequality $y \leq 8$, y represents the number of students a minibus can hold.

    a Is 10 a possible value of x? Explain.

    b Is 7 a possible value of x? Explain.

    c Draw a number line to represent the solution set of the inequality. State the maximum number of students the minibus can hold.

Each inequality has the variable on the right side of the inequality symbol. Graph each solution set on a number line.

28 $9\frac{3}{5} \leq m$

29 $-8 \geq n$

30 $6\frac{1}{4} < p$

31 $4.95 > q$

Chapter 8

Extra Practice and Homework
Equations and Inequalities

Activity 5   Real-World Problems: Inequalities

Solve.

1 Jocelyn swam more than 24 laps.

   a Let x represent the number of laps Jocelyn swam. Write an inequality to represent the situation.

   b Is 20 a possible value of x? Explain.

2 The total number of seats in a concert hall is 450. The number of spectators must be less than or equal to the number of seats.

   a Let y represent the number of spectators in a concert. Write an inequality to represent the situation.

   b Is 432 a possible value of y? Explain.

3 The runtime of a movie is more than or equal to 120 minutes.

  a Let p represent the runtime of a movie. Write an inequality to represent the situation.

  b Is 150.25 a possible value of p? Explain.

4 The weight of the passengers a lift can hold is less than 1,200 pounds.

  a Let q represent the weight of the passengers in the lift. Write an inequality to represent the situation.

  b Is $1,234\frac{5}{6}$ a possible value of q? Explain.

5 A toddler is a child from 12 to 36 months old.

    a Write an inequality to describe the possible ages of a toddler.

    b Liam is 11 months old and Jenna is 35 months old. Are they toddlers? Explain.

6 A bookshelf can hold a maximum of 80 comic books. The comic books are bundled together in groups of 4. Write an inequality to find the maximum number of bundles of comic books that the shelf can hold.

7 The width of a rectangle is 12 inches. What must the length be if the perimeter is at least 96 inches?

8 In order to get a bonus this month, Henry must sell at least 150 newspaper subscriptions. He sold 95 subscriptions in the first two weeks of the month. How many subscriptions must Henry sell in the last two weeks of the month?

Mathematical Habit 3 Construct viable arguments

Brian solved the following equation.

$$
\begin{aligned}
6 - 4.5x &= 1.5 \\
6 - 4.5x + 6 &= 1.5 + 6 \\
-4.5x &= 7.5 \\
x &= 7.5 - 4.5 \\
&= 3
\end{aligned}
$$

Comment whether Brian has solved the equation correctly. If not, explain his mistakes.

Mathematical Habit 1 Persevere in solving problems

The diagram shows a rectangle. The perimeter of the rectangle is at most 32 inches.

$(2x + 1)$ in.

x in.

a Write an inequality for the width of the rectangle.

b Write an inequality for the length of the rectangle.

c Given that x is an integer, list all the possible values of the width of the rectangle and the corresponding values of the length of the rectangle.

Extra Practice and Homework
The Coordinate Plane

Activity 1   Points on a Coordinate Plane

Use the coordinate plane provided.

1. Give the coordinates of each point. In which quadrant is each point located?

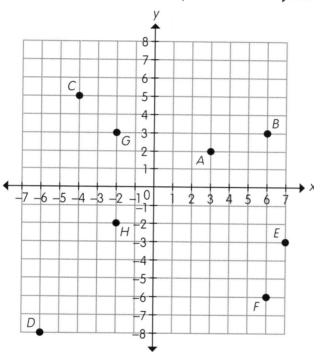

2. Plot the points $A(2, -3)$, $B(5, 5)$, $C(-5, 7)$, $D(-6, -7)$, $E(5, -4)$, $F(1, -7)$, $G(-2, 4)$, and $H(3, -5)$ on the coordinate plane below. In which quadrant is each point located?

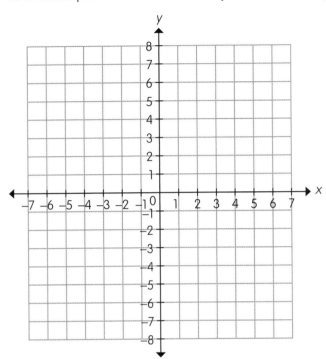

3. Points J and K are reflections of each other about the x-axis. Use the coordinate plane below. Give the coordinates of point K if the coordinates of point J are the following:

a $(2, 4)$ b $(-4, 5)$ c $(6, -2)$ d $(-7, -3)$

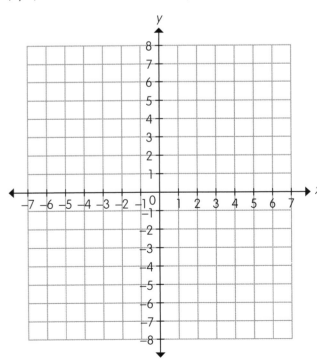

4 Points *M* and *N* are reflections of each other about the *y*-axis. Use the coordinate plane below. Give the coordinates of point *N* if the coordinates of point *M* are the following:

a (3, 5)   b (−3, 6)   c (4, −3)   d (−6, −7)

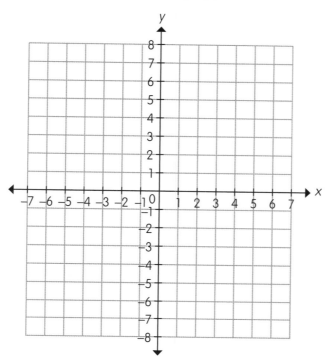

Plot the given points on a coordinate plane. Then, connect the points in order with line segments to form a closed figure. Name each figure formed.

5 *A*(−4, −2), *B*(4, −2), *C*(4, 6), and *D*(−4, 6)

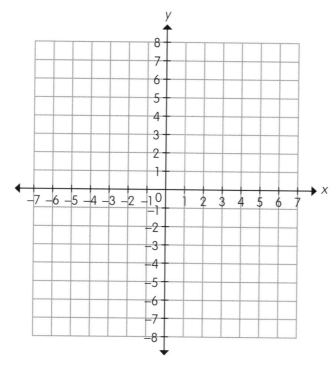

6 $A(0, 5)$, $B(3, -3)$, and $C(5, 1)$

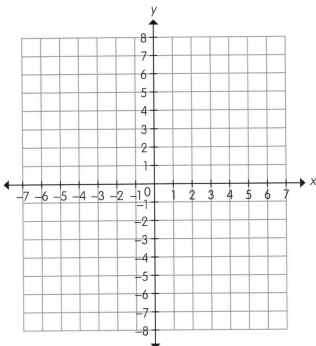

7 $A(0, 0)$, $B(4, 3)$, $C(3, 6)$, and $D(-1, 3)$

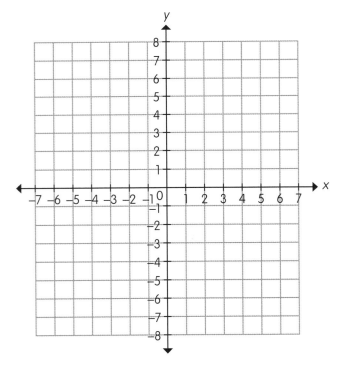

Plot the points on a coordinate plane and answer each question.

8 **a** Plot Points $E(-2, -4)$, $F(4, -4)$, and $G(1, 5)$ on a coordinate plane.

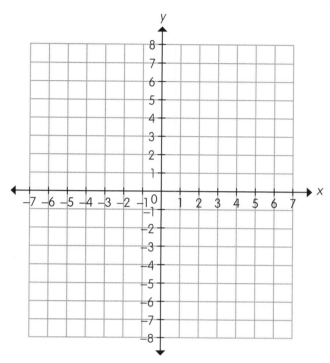

b What kind of triangle is triangle *EFG*?

c Figure *EFGH* is a parallelogram. Plot point *H* and give its coordinates.

9 **a** Plot Points P(−5, 3), and R(3, −3) on a coordinate plane.

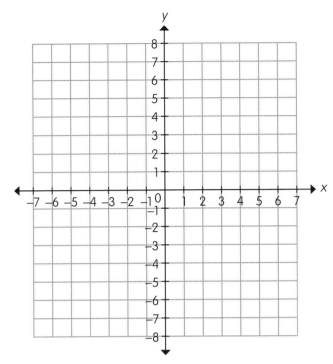

b Join Points P and R with a line segment.

c $\overline{PR}$ is the diagonal of Rectangle PQRS. Point Q is (3, 3). Find the coordinates of point S.

Chapter 9

Extra Practice and Homework
The Coordinate Plane

Activity 2   Lengths of Line Segments

Plot each pair of points on a coordinate plane. Connect the points to form a line segment and find its length.

1 A(3, 1) and B(3, −4)

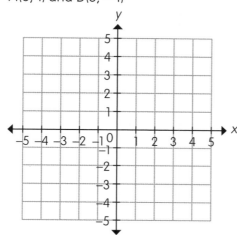

2 C(−5, 0) and D(4, 0)

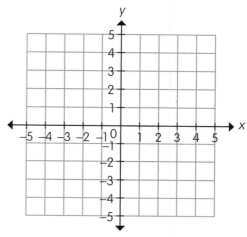

3 E(−4, 2) and F(5, 2)

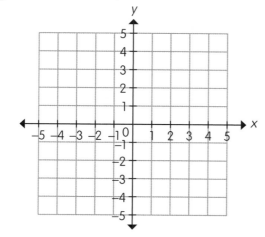

4 G(−3, 4) and H(−3, −3)

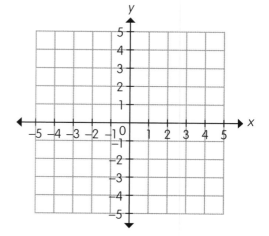

Solve.

5 Rectangle *PQRS* is plotted on a coordinate plane. The coordinates of point *P* are (2, −2), and the coordinates of point *S* are (2, 4). Each unit on the coordinate plane represents 1 centimeter, and the perimeter of Rectangle *PQRS* is 18 centimeters. Find the coordinates of points *Q* and *R* given these conditions:

a Points *Q* and *R* are to the right of Points *P* and *S*.

b Points *Q* and *R* are to the left of Points *P* and *S*.

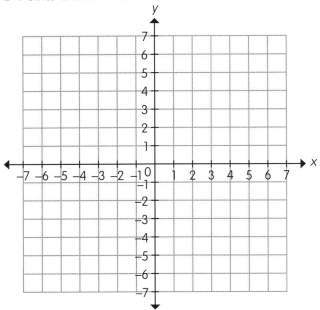

6 Square *ABCD* is plotted on a coordinate plane. The coordinates of point *A* are (−1, 2) and the coordinates of point *B* are (2, 2). Find the coordinates of points *C* and *D* given these conditions:

a Points *C* and *D* are above points *A* and *B*.

b Points *C* and *D* are below points *A* and *B*.

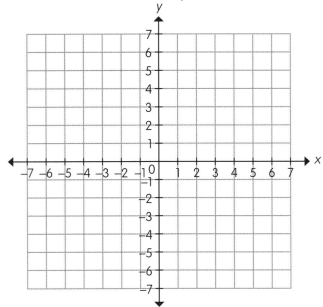

In the diagram, Triangle *EFG* represents the outline of a plot of land. The side length of each grid square is 1 mile. Use the diagram to answer ⑦ to ⑩.

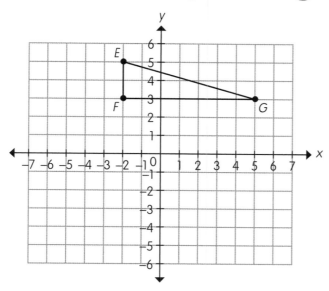

⑦ Triangle *EFG* is plotted on a coordinate plane. Write the coordinates of Points *E*, *F*, and *G*.

⑧ What type of triangle is triangle *EFG*?

⑨ Find the area of triangle *EFG*.

⑩ Figure *EFGH* is a rectangle. Plot point *H* on the coordinate plane and give its coordinates.

In the diagram, figure *ABCDEF* represents the base of a building. The side length of each grid square is 5 feet. Use the diagram to answer ⑪ to ⑭.

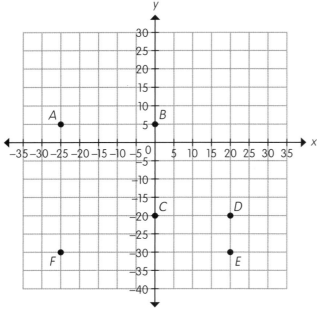

⑪ Give the coordinates of points *A, B, C, D, E,* and *F*.

⑫ Brian and Carter built a fence around the building. They left a 5-foot opening for the gate. What is the total length of the fence?

⑬ The gate, *GH*, lies on *CD* and is 10 feet from point *D*. Give the coordinates of points *G* and *H*.

⑭ Find the area the building occupies.

Chapter 9

Extra Practice and Homework
The Coordinate Plane

Activity 3   Real-World Problems: Graphing

Solve.

1 There is a $35 annual fee for membership at the gym. It also costs $10 per visit to use the gym. Fill in the table to show the cost, *y* dollars, of *x* visits to the gym. Graph the relationship between *y* and *x*. Use 2 units on the horizontal axis to represent 1 visit and 1 unit on the vertical axis to represent $10.

Number of Visits to Gym (x)	1	2	3	4	5
Cost of Visiting Gym ($y)	45	55			

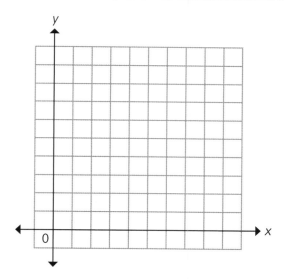

a   How much will it cost to visit the gym 5 times?

b   Name the dependent and independent variables.

2 The number of portraits, *p*, that an artist can draw in *t* hours is given by $p = 5t$. Fill in the table. Graph this relationship between *p* and *t*. Use 2 units on the horizontal axis to represent 1 hour and 1 unit on the vertical axis to represent 5 portraits.

Time (*t* h)	1	2	3	4	5
Number of Portraits (*p*)	5		15		

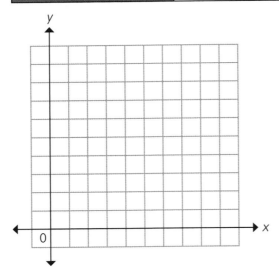

a What type of graph is it?

b How many portraits can the artist paint in 4 hours?

c How long will it take the artist to paint 25 portraits?

d If the artist has to paint at least 32 figurines, how many hours will she need to paint? Express your answer in the form of an inequality in terms of *h*.

3 Water is drained from a pool. The water level, *y* centimeters, at time *x* minutes, is given by $y = 40 - 5x$. Complete the table. Graph the relationship between *x* and *y*. Use 1 unit on the horizontal axis to represent 1 minute and 1 unit on the vertical axis to represent 10 centimeters.

Time (x min)	2	4	6	8
Water Level (y cm)	30			

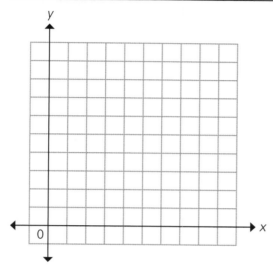

a What is the water level at 3 minutes?

b In how many minutes will the water level be 15 centimeters?

c How long will it take to drain all the water from the pool?

d What is the average drainage rate of the pool?

4. The fee, f dollars, a certain plumber charges is given by $f = 30t + 10$, where t is the number of hours the plumber spends on the job. Fill in the table. Graph the relationship between f and t. Use 2 units on the horizontal axis to represent 1 hour and 1 unit on the vertical axis to represent \$20.

Time (t h)	0	1	2	3	4
Fee Charged (\$$f$)	10	40			

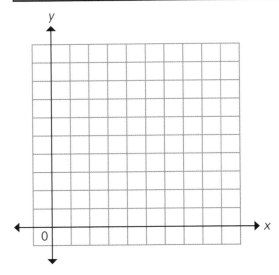

a What is the fee charged by the plumber if he spends 4 hours on the job?

b How many hours does the plumber spend on the job if his fee is \$70?

c How long does the plumber spend on the job in order for him to earn a fee of more than \$100?

d What is the average fee the plumber earns per hour?

Mathematical Habit 2 **Use mathematical reasoning**

In real life, we study the relationship between two quantities. When two quantities are related by a linear equation, we can gather many useful information. Explain the importance of studying linear relationship between two quantities.

Mathematical Habit 5 Use tools strategically

For **a** to **c**, plot each set of points on a coordinate plane. Then, join the points in order with line segments to form a closed figure and label it. Name each figure formed.

a $A(-2, 0)$, $B(0, -2)$, $C(2, 0)$, $D(0, 2)$

b $E(-4, 0)$, $F(0, -4)$, $G(4, 0)$, $H(0, 4)$

c $J(-6, 0)$, $K(0, -6)$, $M(6, 0)$, $N(0, 6)$

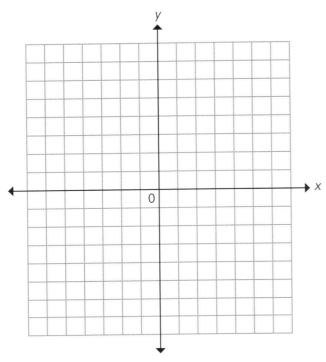

d Find the area of figures *ABCD*, *EFGH*, and *JKMN* if each unit on the coordinate plane represents 1 inch.

e What conclusion can you draw about the relationship among the areas of figures *ABCD*, *EFGH*, and *JKMN*?

Chapter 10

Extra Practice and Homework
Area of Polygons

Activity 1   Area of Triangles

Identify a base, *b*, and its corresponding height, *h*, for each triangle.

 1

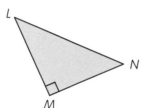

 2

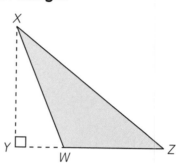

Label a base, *b*, and a height, *h*, of each triangle.

 3

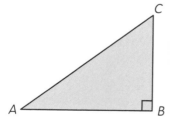

4

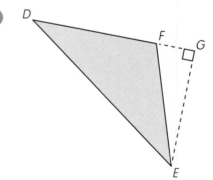

There can be more than one way to label the base and the height of a triangle.

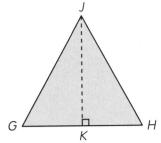

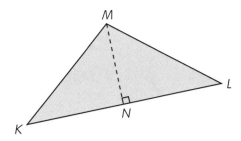

Find the area of each triangle.

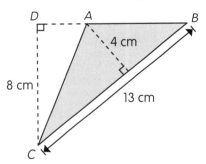

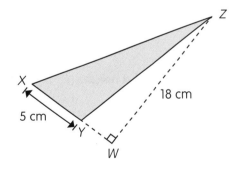

The area of each triangle is 126 square centimeters. Find the height of each triangle and round your answer to the nearest tenth of a centimeter.

9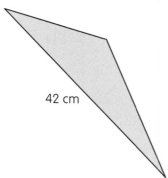

42 cm

10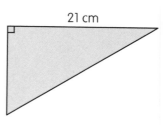

21 cm

The area of each triangle is 108 square inches. Find the height of each triangle and round your answer to the nearest tenth of an inch.

11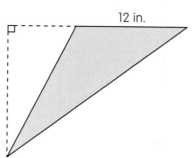

12 in.

12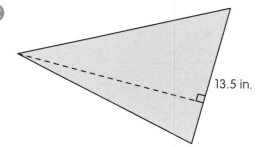

13.5 in.

Find the area of each shaded region.

13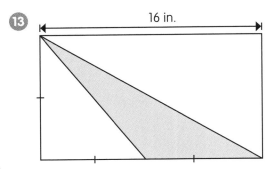

14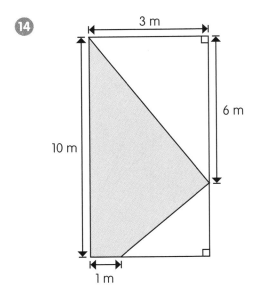

15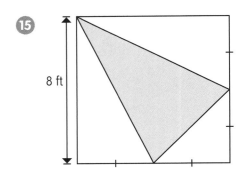

16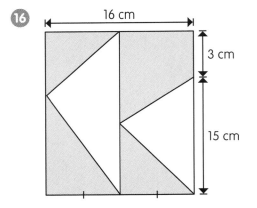

Solve.

17 The coordinates of the vertices of a triangle are $J(3, 2)$, $K(-1, 2)$, and $L(-1, -5)$. Find the area of triangle JKL.

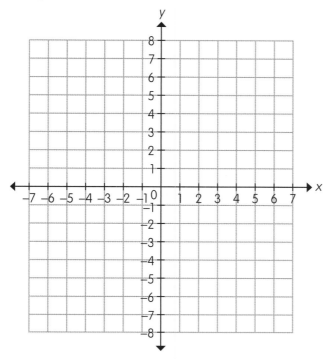

18 The coordinates of the vertices of a triangle are $M(6, -2)$, $N(6, 5)$, and $O(-2, -2)$. Find the area of triangle MNO.

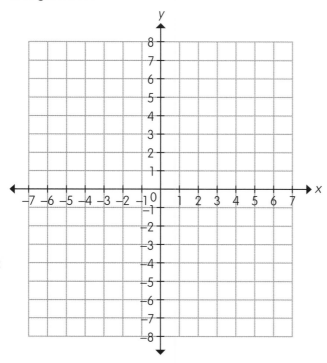

19 The coordinates of the vertices of a triangle are $P(-6, 6)$, $Q(-6, -1)$, and $R(5, -1)$. Find the area of triangle PQR.

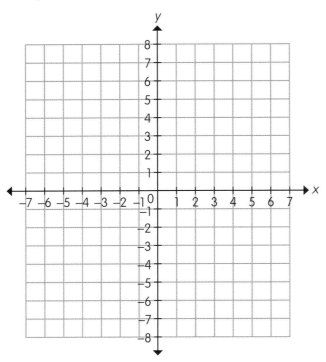

20 The area of Triangle XYZ is 22.5 square units. The coordinates of X are $(2, 5)$ and the coordinates of Y are $(-3, -4)$. The height of Triangle XYZ is 9 units and is parallel to the y-axis. Point Z lies to the right of Point Y. Given that $\overline{YZ}$ is the base of the triangle, find the coordinates of Point Z.

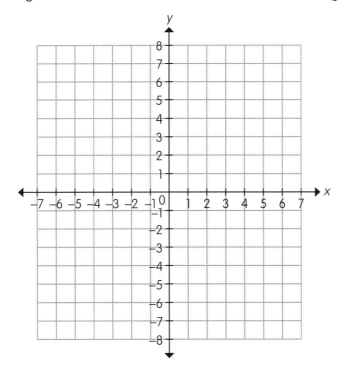

21 The coordinates of the vertices of a triangle are $A(-2, 6)$, $B(-2, -3)$, and $C(4, -1)$. Find the area of triangle ABC. (Hint: Use the vertical side as the base.)

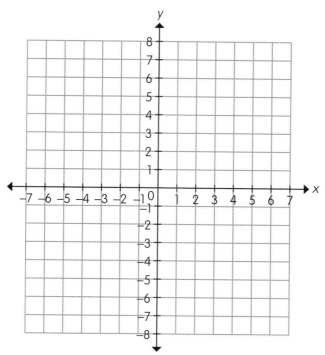

22 The coordinates of the vertices of a triangle are $P(1, -5)$, $Q(3, 4)$, and $R(-2, -2)$. Find the area of triangle PQR. (Hint: Draw a rectangle around Triangle PQR.)

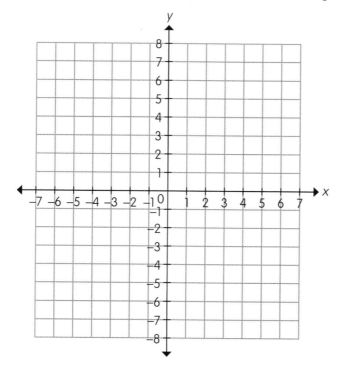

Find the area of the shaded region.

23 A right triangle has a height of 16 centimeters and a base of 12 centimeters. Four such triangles are arranged to form a large square with a small square at the center, as shown. Find the side length of the large square.

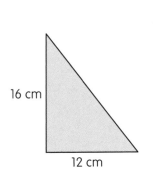

16 cm

12 cm

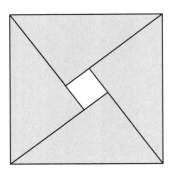

Find the total area of the 4 shaded triangles and the small square.

Chapter 10

Extra Practice and Homework
Area of Polygons

Activity 2   Area of Parallelograms and Trapezoids

Label a base, *b*, and a height, *h*, for each parallelogram. Use *b* and *h*.

1

A   D

B   C

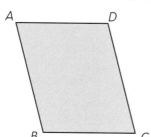

2

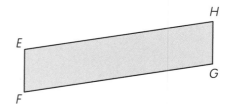

E   H   G   F

3

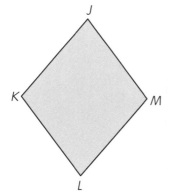

J

K   M

L

4

S

P

Q   R

Find the area of each parallelogram.

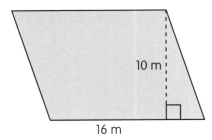

10 m

16 m

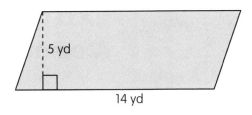

5 yd

14 yd

Label bases, b_1 and b_2, and a height, h, of each trapezoid. Use b_1, b_2, and h.

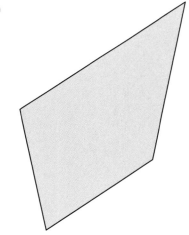

9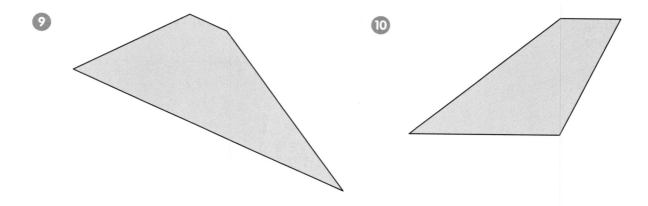

10

Find the area of each trapezoid.

11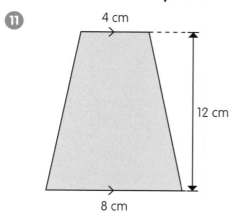

4 cm

12 cm

8 cm

12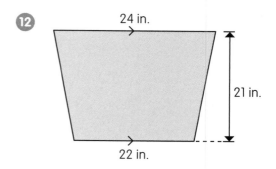

24 in.

21 in.

22 in.

Draw straight lines to divide each figure into polygons. Describe two ways to find the area of each figure.

13

14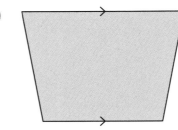

Draw straight lines to divide each figure into polygons. Describe a way to find the area of each figure.

15

16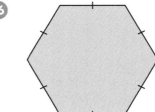

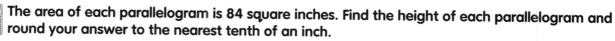 The area of each parallelogram is 84 square inches. Find the height of each parallelogram and round your answer to the nearest tenth of an inch.

17

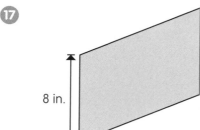

8 in.

18

3.5 in.

The area of each trapezoid is 105 square centimeters. Find the height of each parallelogram and round your answer to the nearest tenth of a centimeter.

19

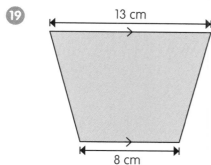

13 cm

8 cm

20

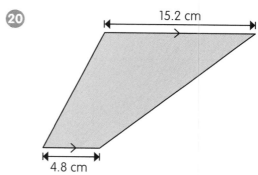

15.2 cm

4.8 cm

Solve.

21 Parallelogram *ABDE* is made up of Rectangle *ACDF*, Triangle *ABC*, and Triangle *FDE*. The ratio of the length of $\overline{CD}$ to the length of $\overline{BC}$ is 8 : 1. Triangles *ABC* and *FDE* are identical and the height of each triangle is 7 inches. The area of Triangle *ABC* is 14 square meters. Find the area of Parallelogram *ABDE*.

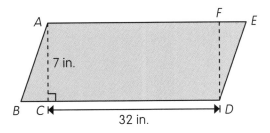

22 Parallelogram *PQRS* is made up of Isosceles Triangle *RST* and Trapezoid *PQRT*. Find the area of Parallelogram *PQRS*.

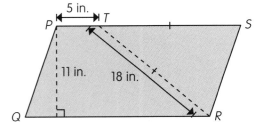

23 The area of Trapezoid *CDEF* is 175 square centimeters. Find the area of Triangle *CDF*.

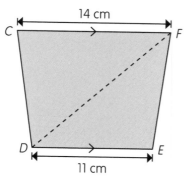

24 Trapezoid *RSTU* is made up of three triangles and Triangle *TUV* is an isosceles triangle. Find the area of Trapezoid *RSTV* if the area of Trapezoid *RSTU* is 513 square centimeters.

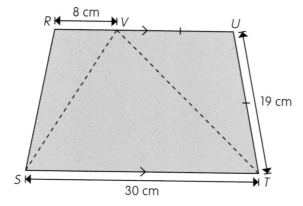

25 The coordinates of the vertices of a parallelogram are $A(-3, 1)$, $B(-5, -2)$, $C(0, -2)$, and $D(2, 1)$. Find the area of Parallelogram $ABCD$.

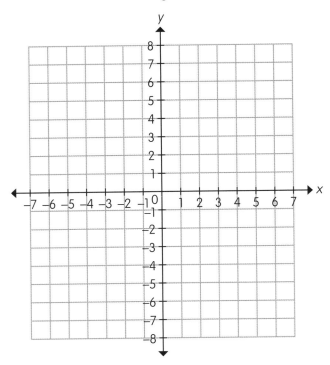

26 Three out of the four coordinates of the vertices of a parallelogram are $E(3, 2)$, $F(-1, 2)$, and $G(-4, 5)$. Plot the coordinates on the coordinate plane. Find the coordinates of point H. Then, find the area of Parallelogram $EFGH$.

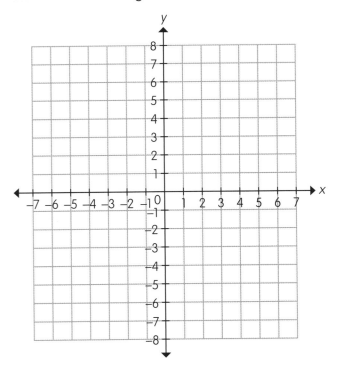

27 The coordinates of the vertices of a trapezoid are $J(-4, 4)$, $K(-6, -2)$, $L(3, -2)$, and $M(1, 4)$. Plot the coordinates on the coordinate plane. Find the area of Trapezoid $JKLM$.

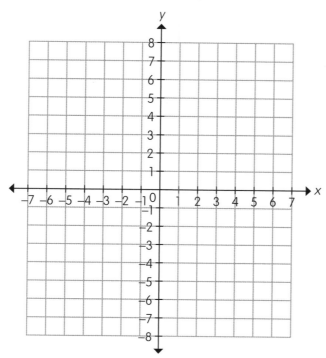

28 Three out of the four coordinates of the vertices of Trapezoid $PQRS$ are $P(4, 3)$, $Q(1, -3)$, and $R(-2, -3)$. $\overline{QR}$ is parallel to $\overline{PS}$. The length of $\overline{PS}$ is 10 units. Point S lies to the left of Point P. Find the coordinates of Point S. Then, find the area of the trapezoid.

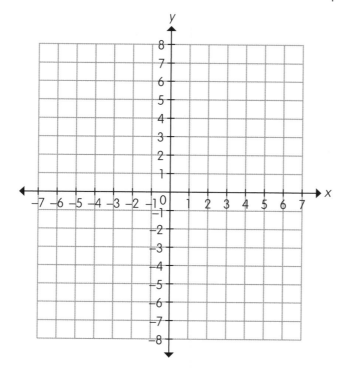

29 **a** Plot Points $V(-3, -1)$, $W(-3, -3)$, $X(2, -3)$, $Y(6, 0)$, and $Z(1, 2)$ on a coordinate plane. Join the points in order to form Figure $VWXYZ$.

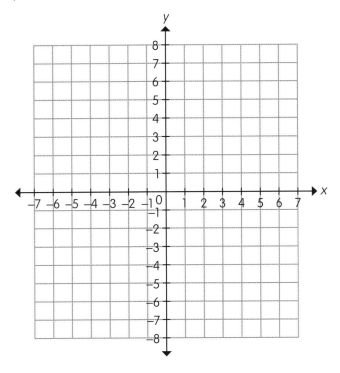

b Find the area of Figure $VWXYZ$.

Draw a rectangle around figure $VWXYZ$.

c Find the area of Figure $WXYZ$.

Chapter 10

Extra Practice and Homework
Area of Polygons

Activity 3   Area of Other Polygons

Find the area of each kite.

 1

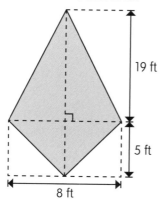

19 ft

5 ft

8 ft

2

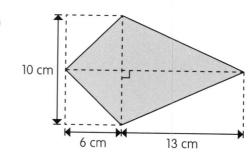

10 cm

6 cm   13 cm

Divide each regular polygon into identical triangles. Write the minimum number of triangles you could obtain.

 3

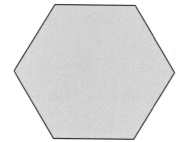

4

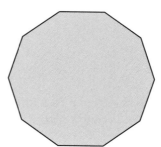

Solve.

5 A regular hexagon is formed by 3 identical rhombuses. The height of each rhombus is 8 meters and its base is 10 meters. Find the area of the hexagon.

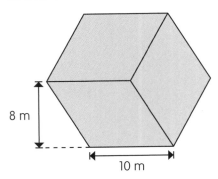

8 m

10 m

6 A clock frame in the shape of a regular hexagon has an area of 187.2 square inches. The length of each side of the hexagonal clock is 12 inches. Find the height of the clock.

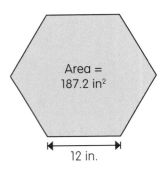

Area = 187.2 in²

12 in.

7 A carpet in the shape of a regular pentagon has an area of 2,940 square centimeters. Find the length of each side of the carpet.

28 cm

Find the area of each regular polygon.

8 The shaded area is 40.8 square inches.

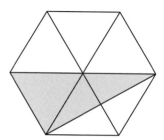

9 The shaded area is 453.6 square centimeters.

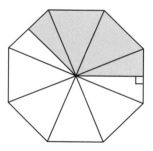

Each figure is made up of a regular polygon surrounded by identical triangles. Find the area of each figure.

10

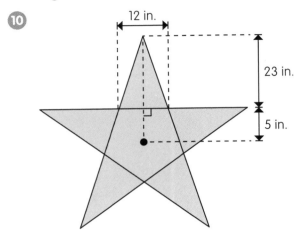

11

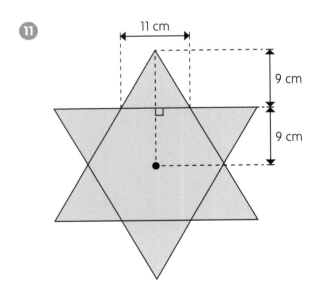

Mathematical Habit 2 Use mathematical reasoning

Layla drew two triangles, A and B, using the same line $\overline{XY}$ as the base of the triangles. She concluded that both triangles have the same area. Do you agree? Explain your answer.

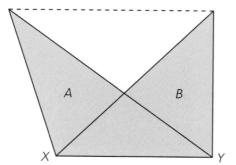

1 **Mathematical Habit** **7** **Make use of structure**

Figure *PQRS* is a square of side length 14 centimeters. Find the shaded area of the figure.

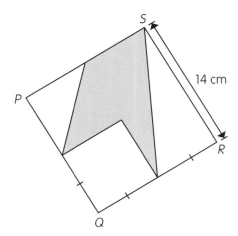

2 **Mathematical Habit** **1** **Persevere in solving problems**

In the diagram, figure *ABFE* is a parallelogram. Its area is 240 square centimeters. The length of $\overline{AB}$ is 13 centimeters and the length of $\overline{BD}$ is 30 centimeters. Given that the length of $\overline{FD}$ is $\frac{1}{3}$ that of the length of $\overline{BD}$, calculate the area of trapezoid *ABDE*.

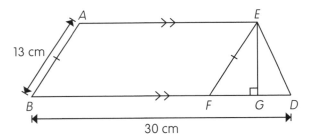

Chapter 11

Extra Practice and Homework
Surface Area and Volume of Solids

Activity 1　Prisms and Pyramids

Name each solid. In each solid, identify a base and a face that is not a base.

1

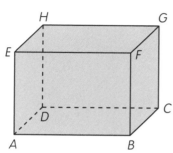

2

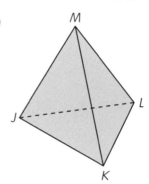

3

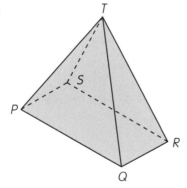

4

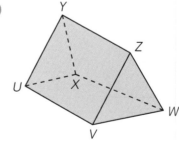

Name the solid that each net forms.

 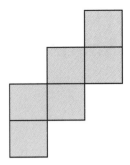

 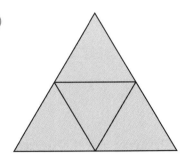

 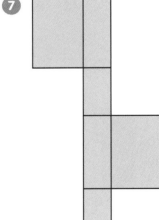

 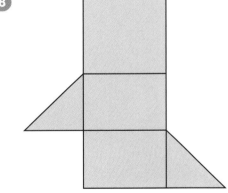

Extra Practice and Homework Course 1B

Solve.

9 The base of a prism has p vertices. Write an expression for each statement.

a The number of sides of the base of the prism

b The number of edges of the prism

c The number of faces of the prism

10 A pyramid has q faces. Write an expression for each statement.

a The number of sides of the base of the pyramid

b The number of edges of the pyramid

c The number of vertices of the pyramid

Decide whether each figure will form a cube. Answer Yes or No.

⑪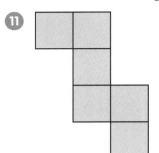

⑫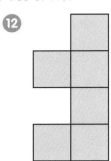

⑬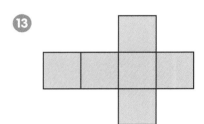

⑭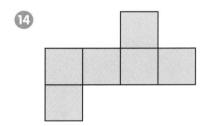

Solve.

⑮ In ⑪ to ⑭, you identified some possible nets of a cube. There are other possible nets. Draw two other possible nets.

Decide whether each figure will form a prism. Answer Yes or No.

16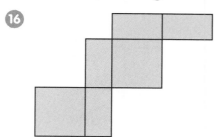

17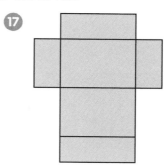

18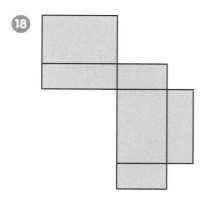

19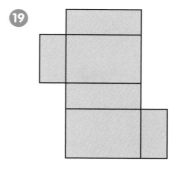

The net of each solid figure is shown below. Write the missing vertices.

20

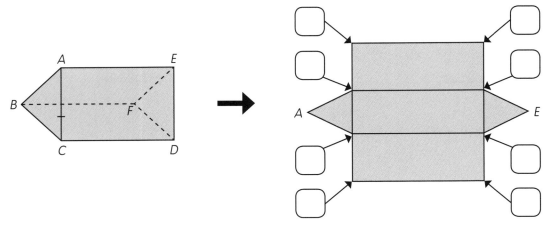

21

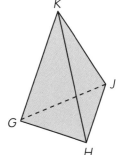

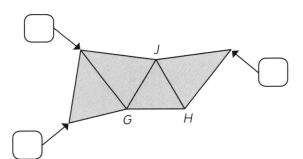

Chapter 11

Extra Practice and Homework
Surface Area and Volume of Solids

Activity 2   Surface Area of Solids

Find the surface area of each cube.

1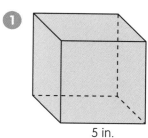

5 in.

2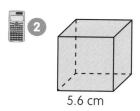

5.6 cm

Find the surface area of each rectangular prism.

3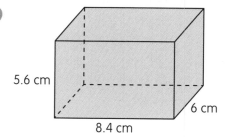

5.6 cm

8.4 cm

6 cm

4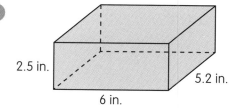

2.5 in.

6 in.

5.2 in.

Find the surface area of each triangular prism.

 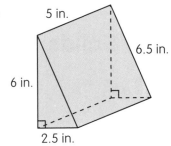

5 in.

6.5 in.

6 in.

2.5 in.

 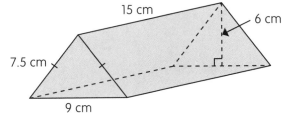

15 cm

6 cm

7.5 cm

9 cm

Solve.

7 A rectangular shipping container measures 6 feet by 10 feet by 4 feet. Find the surface area of the shipping container.

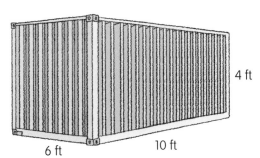

4 ft

6 ft

10 ft

8 A triangular prism with its measurements is shown. Find the surface area of the prism.

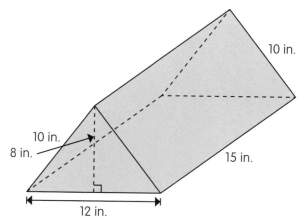

9 A piece of cake in the shape of a triangular prism is shown below. Find the surface area of the cake.

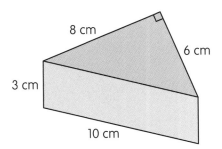

Chapter 11

Extra Practice and Homework
Surface Area and Volume of Solids

Activity 3 Volume of Rectangular Prisms

Find the volume of each cube.

1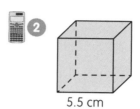

9 in.

2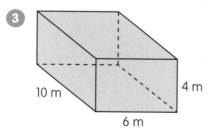

5.5 cm

Find the volume of each rectangular prism.

3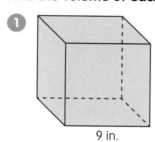

10 m
6 m
4 m

4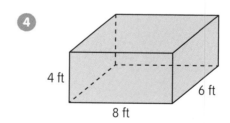

4 ft
8 ft
6 ft

Solve.

5 Find the volume of the chocolate box.

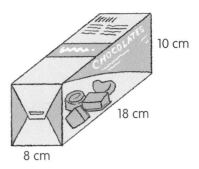

10 cm

18 cm

8 cm

6 A cube has edges measuring 7 inches each. Find the volume of the cube.

7 The solid below is made of identical cubes. Each cube has an edge length of 2 inches. Find the volume of the solid.

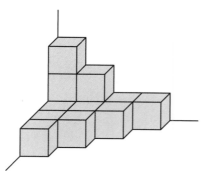

8 The volume of a rectangular prism with square bases is 2,916 cubic inches. The base has a side length of 6 inches. Find the height of the prism.

9　A water tank is 80 centimeters long and 50 centimeters wide. What is the volume of water in the tank given that the height of water is 30 centimeters?

10　How many 2-centimeter cubes are needed to fill the rectangular box completely?

14 cm

20 cm

32 cm

Chapter 11

Extra Practice and Homework
Surface Area and Volume of Solids

Activity 4   Real-World Problems: Surface Area and Volume

Solve.

1 A rectangular pool 60 meters by 25 meters by 4 meters deep is $\frac{1}{4}$ full of water.

    a Find the volume of water needed to fill the pool completely.

    b Find the volume of water needed to fill $\frac{2}{3}$ of the pool.

2 The volume of Box X is $\frac{1}{4}$ the volume of Box Y. Box Y is a cube of side length 10 centimeters. What is the height of Box X if it has a base area of 16 square centimeters?

3. A rectangular prism and a cube have the same volume. The rectangular prism measures 18 inches by 16 inches by 6 inches. Find the length of each side of the cube.

4. An open box is 10 inches long, 8 inches wide, and 3 inches tall. The outer surface area of the box is painted with blue paint. Find the surface area of the box that is painted.

5. A container is in the shape of a square prism. The container is 12 inches high, and its volume is 588 cubic inches.

   a Find the length of each side of the square base.

   b Find the surface area of the container.

6 A rectangular tank with a square base is $\frac{1}{2}$ full of water. The side length of the square base is 10 inches. When another 300 cubic inches of water is poured into the tank, it becomes $\frac{2}{3}$ full.

a Find the capacity of the tank.

b When the tank is $\frac{2}{3}$ full, what is the height of the water level?

Mathematical Habit 4 Use mathematical models

A cuboid tank measures 13 inches by 27 inches by 20 inches. Christian says that the maximum number of 3-inch cubes that can be put into the cuboid tank is 260. Do you agree with Christian? Explain your answer.

PUT ON YOUR THINKING CAP!

1 **Mathematical Habit 1** **Persevere in solving problems**

A solid is made by removing a smaller rectangular prism from a larger rectangular prism. Both prisms have square bases. The side length of the square base of the smaller prism is 5 centimeters. The side length of the square base of the larger prism is 16 centimeters. Find the volume of the solid.

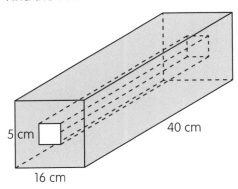

2 **Mathematical Habit 1** **Persevere in solving problems**

A triangular prism is cut from a 10-centimeter cube as shown in the diagram. *A, B, C* and *D* are corners of the cube. *BX* is 6 centimeters and *BY* is 8 centimeters.

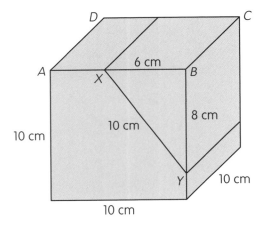

Calculate

a the volume of the triangular prism removed,

b the area of the cross section of the solid which remains,

c the total surface area of the solid which remains.

Chapter 12

Extra Practice and Homework
Introduction to Statistics

Activity 1 Collecting and Tabulating Data

Decide if each sentence is a statistical question. Answer Yes or No.

1 Who keeps cats or dogs as pets?

2 What is the tallest building in the world?

3 How many of each type of animals are there in the zoo?

4 What is the number of students in each class?

5 What is your favorite food?

6 How many of your classmates either take bus or cycle to school?

Answer each question.

7 A fruit seller conducted a survey. He asked their customers to state their favorite fruits. A tally chart was used to record his findings.

Fruit	Tally	Frequency
Apple	卌 |||	
Orange	卌 ||||	
Strawberry	卌 卌 |||	
Grape	卌	

a How many customers took part in the survey?

b How many more customers prefer strawberries to apples?

c What percent of the customers surveyed stated grapes as their favorite?

8   Some students were asked to name their favorite subject. The table shows their responses.

Subject	Tally	Frequency
Physical Education	‖‖ ‖‖	
Music	‖‖‖	
English	‖‖ ‖	
Science	‖‖ ‖‖	

a How many students were asked?

b How many students named Music or English as their favorite subject?

c What fraction of the students named Science as their favorite subject?

9 The number of flowers in the garden was counted and the flowers are grouped based on their colors as shown in the table.

Subject	Tally	Frequency
Red	卌	
Yellow	卌	
White	卌 |||	
Orange	||	

a How many flowers were counted?

b How many flowers were yellow or white?

c What percent of the flowers were red?

10 Mr. Cox wanted to find out how many hours in a day his students spend surfing the Internet. The average number of hours reported by each student is as shown.

```
1 3 3 4 2 0 2 2 2
2 3 5 4 3 5 3 3 3
6 6 3 5 6 3 4 5 6
```

a Arrange the numbers in ascending order.

b Complete the frequency table.

Number of Hours	Tally	Frequency
0–2		
3–4		
5–6		

c How many students spend more than 2 hours each day surfing the Internet?

d How many students spend less than 5 hours each day surfing the Internet?

11 Grace conducted a survey among 30 families in her neighborhood. She asked them the number of pets in their household. The data she collected is as shown.

2	1	3	2	2	0	3	1	0	4
0	2	2	1	3	2	4	0	1	1
3	2	2	1	1	1	0	0	3	2

a Arrange the numbers in ascending order.

b Complete the frequency table.

Number of Pets	Tally	Frequency
0–1		
2–3		
4–5		

c How many families owned at least 2 pets?

d What percent of the families owned 4 to 5 pets?

Extra Practice and Homework Course 1B

Extra Practice and Homework
Introduction to Statistics

Activity 2   Dot Plots

Draw a dot plot for each set of data.

1 A group of 20 students were asked the number of hours they exercised each day. The number of hours is as shown.

1	2	3	4	5	0	1	4	2	2
5	4	3	3	2	3	2	2	3	4

2 A group of 27 students were asked the number of soft toys they owned. The number of soft toys is as shown.

Number of Soft Toys	0	1	2	3	4
Freqeuncy	6	10	6	3	2

Answer each question.

3 The dot plot shows the number of books a group of students read last month.

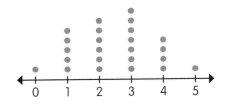

a Find the number of students surveyed.

b From the dot plot, what can you tell about the number of books the students read?

c What percent of the students read at least 3 books?

4 The dot plot shows the number of movies a group of children watched in a year.

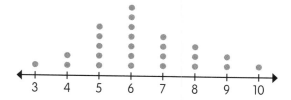

a Find the number of children surveyed.

b From the dot plot, what can you tell about the number of movies the children watched?

c What percent of the children watched at least 8 movies?

5 The dot plot shows the number of sports some students played.

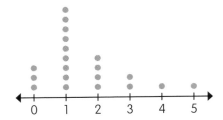

a Find the number of students surveyed.

b What percent of the students played less than 2 sports?

c A few more students were surveyed and all of them played less than 2 sports. Of all of the students surveyed, $\frac{5}{7}$ of them played less than 2 sports. How many more students were surveyed?

Chapter 12

Extra Practice and Homework
Introduction to Statistics

Activity 3   Histograms

Draw a histogram for each set of data. Include a title.

1 The table shows the number of rounds a runner completed around the track in a month.

Number of Rounds	1–2	3–4	5–6	7–8	9–10
Freqeuncy	1	3	6	8	9

2 The table shows the number of bus services that serves different towns.

Number of Bus Services	1–3	4–6	7–9	10–12
Freqeuncy	5	6	4	1

3 The table shows the number of goals by a basketball player in a season.

Number of Goals	0–1	2–3	4-5	6–7	8–9
Freqeuncy	2	6	7	8	3

4 The table shows the number of books read by some students in a month.

Number of Books Read	0–1	2–3	4–5	6–7	8–9
Freqeuncy	1	4	8	6	3

Solve.

5 The times taken by 25 students to complete a run are shown in the table. The times were rounded to the nearest minute.

Time (min)	31–35	36–40	41–45	46–50	51–55
Freqeuncy	4	p	8	4	3

a Find the value of p.

b Draw a histogram to represent the data. Briefly describe the data.

c What percent of the students took at least 41 minutes to complete their run?

6 The histogram shows the scores of a Math quiz for a group of students.

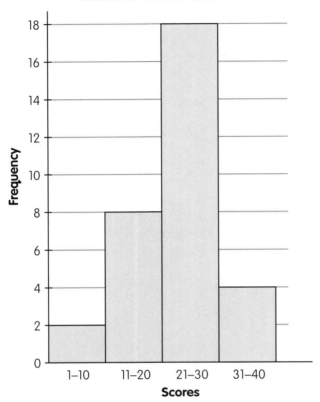

a How many students are there?

b What percent of the students scored at most 30 marks?

c How many fewer students scored from 11 to 20 marks than from 21 to 30 marks?

Mathematical Habit 5 Use tools strategically

Julian wants to record the number of siblings each of his classmates has and the weight of his classmates. Determine whether a dot plot or a histogram is more appropriate to display the data he wants to record. Explain your answer.

Mathematical Habit 1 Persevere in solving problems

The numbers of years some workers have been employed in a company are shown in the table.

Number of Years	0–1	2–3	4–5	6–7	8–9
Freqeuncy	14	13	8	x	10

The ratio of the number of workers who have worked more than 5 years to the number of workers who have worked 5 years or less is 7 : 5.

a Find the total number of workers in the company.

b Find the value of x.

c Draw a histogram to correctly represent the data. Include a title.

d 9 new workers joined the company. What percent of the workers have worked less than 2 years?

Chapter 13

Extra Practice and Homework
Measure of Central Tendency and Variability

Activity 1 Mean

Find the mean of each data set.

1 18, 21, 22, 25, 27, 27, 42

2 30, 32, 31, 33, 35, 44, 36, 38, 37

3 28.4 cm, 31.3 cm, 95.1 cm, 42.2 cm, 64.7 cm, 22.7 cm

Solve.

4 The heights of five moose are 4.8 feet, 6.2 feet, 5.8 feet, 6.0 feet, and 5.6 feet. Find the mean height of these five moose.

5　The amount of time nine paper airplanes stayed in the air are 2.3 seconds, 4.2 seconds, 3.0 seconds, 4.6 seconds, 3.8 seconds, 1.9 seconds, 4.0 seconds, 5.2 seconds, and 5.0 seconds. Find the mean time these nine paper airplanes stayed in the air.

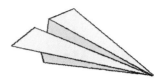

6　The table shows the number of pins that fell in the ten rounds of a bowling game.

Bowling Score

Round Number	1	2	3	4	5	6	7	8	9	10
Number of Pins	8	6	5	8	9	7	8	9	10	8

Find the mean number of pins that fell in the ten rounds of the bowling game.

7 The dot plot shows the number of rackets owned by a group of badminton players.

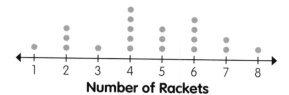

Number of Rackets

a How many players are there in the group?

b Find the total number of rackets.

c Find the mean number of rackets each player owns.

8 The mean of nine numbers is 92. The mean of another three numbers is 26. Find the mean of the combined set of 12 numbers.

9. The mean number of bottles of shampoo in eight boxes is 14. There are 13, 11, 14, 11, 14, 16, and 12 bottles of shampoo in the first seven boxes. Find the number of bottles of shampoo in the last box.

10. The mean height of nine plants is 17 inches. The heights of the first eight plants are 13 inches, 14 inches, 14 inches, 16 inches, 17 inches, 18 inches, 22 inches, and 23 inches. Find the height of the ninth plant.

11. The mean of seven numbers is 53. When one of the numbers is removed, the mean of the remaining six numbers is 46. Find the number that is removed.

12. The mean of six numbers is 43. Four of the numbers are 37, 44, 41, and 52. One of the two unknown numbers is $\frac{3}{4}$ of the other unknown number. Find the two unknown numbers.

13 The mean of eleven numbers is 8. When two of the eleven numbers are removed, the mean of the remaining nine numbers is 7. One of the two numbers that are removed is 5 more than the other number. Find the greater number that is removed.

14 The mean of a set of twelve numbers is 6.5. The mean of another set of eight numbers is k. The mean of the combined set of the 20 numbers is 9.5. Find the value of k.

Chapter 13

Extra Practice and Homework
Measure of Central Tendency and Variability

Activity 2   Median

Find the median of each data set.

1 6, 8, 10, 7, 4, 10, 12

2 36, 38, 29, 27, 39, 33, 36, 41, 31, 29

3 4.5, 5.8, 3.6, 6.6, 9.4, 7.5, 3.4, 10.5, 7.3

4 $5\frac{1}{3}$, $4\frac{3}{5}$, $5\frac{2}{5}$, $4\frac{2}{3}$, $6\frac{5}{12}$, $5\frac{1}{4}$

Solve.

⑤ A shop has 13 pairs of shoes for sale. The sizes include 8, 12, 10, 8, 10, 12, 14, 8, 10, 12, 14, 16, and 10. Find the median size of the pairs of shoes for sale.

⑥ The number of fish caught by 12 competitors in a fishing competition is 8, 6, 3, 7, 4, 7, 6, 4, 9, 5, 6, and 3. Find the median number of fish caught.

© 2020 Marshall Cavendish Education Pte Ltd

7 The dot plot shows the number of countries visited by each student in a class. Each dot represents one student.

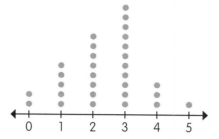

a Find the total number of students.

 b What is the mean number of countries visited by each student? Round your answer to the nearest tenth.

c Find the median number of countries visited.

d Alyssa says that both the mean and the median are good estimates for the data set? Do you agree? Justify your answer.

8 The median of a set of some numbers is x. There are at least three numbers in the set. Write an algebraic expression, in terms of x, to represent the median of the new set of numbers obtained by

a adding $\frac{1}{6}$ to every number in the set.

b subtracting $7\frac{1}{4}$ from every number in the set.

c multiplying -4.9 to every number in the set and then adding 7 to the resulting numbers.

d dividing every number in the set by 0.25 and then subtracting 3 from the resulting numbers.

e adding 9.4 to the greatest number in the set.

f subtracting 6.3 from the least number in the set.

9 The median of a set of eight numbers is 59. The seven numbers are 24, 54, 45, 63, 73, 84, 91, and q. Find the value of q.

10 The median of a set of twelve numbers is 38. The twelve numbers are 43, 41, 31, 41, 39, 33, 40, 36, 43, 35, 34, and b. Find the value of b.

The following data set shows a set of 11 numbers.

8, 7, 4, 10, 12, 11, 6, 11, 6, x, y

The mean and median of the set of numbers is 9. The value of x is less than the value of y. Find the value of x and of y.

Extra Practice and Homework
Measure of Central Tendency and Variability

Activity 3   Mode

Find the mode or modes of each data set.

1 8, 6, 9, 6, 7, 7, 6, 5, 6

2 23, 24, 26, 23, 26, 27, 23, 28, 23

3 9.3, 7.5, 5.8, 8.9, 10.5, 7.5, 7.5, 11.5, 9.3, 10.5, 8.9, 8.9

4 5.6, 4.5, 2.7, 4.3, 4.5, 5.6, 2.7, 5.6, 3.5, 2.7, 3.5, 2.7

Find the mode.

5 The dot plot shows the number of long jumpers in some track and field teams. Each dot represents one team.

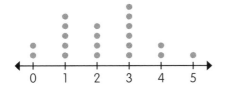

6 The table shows the favorite fruit of a group of students.

Fruit	Number of Students
Apple	9
Avocado	13
Grape	8
Orange	16
Pear	21

Solve.

7 The data set shows the number of oranges on each tree on a plot of land.

102	101	102	102	103	102	101
101	104	104	101	102	103	101
102	105	104	102	103	104	101

a Draw a dot plot to show the data.

 b What is the mean number of oranges? Round your answer to the nearest whole number.

c What is the median number of oranges?

d What is the modal number of oranges?

8 The table shows the mass of 25 dogs measured to the nearest kilogram.

Mass of 25 Dogs

Mass of Dog (kg)	12	13	14	15	16	17	18
Frequency	6	4	5	3	2	1	4

a Draw a dot plot to show the data.

b Find the mean mass of the dogs.

c Find the median mass of the dogs.

d Find the modal mass of the dogs.

9 The ages of 29 children in a choir are listed in the data set. The minimum age to participate in the choir is 8 years old. The maximum age is 13 years old.

12, 9, 11, 9, 13, 12, 13, 10, 10, 11, 13, 11, 11, 9, 11,
11, 12, 10, 12, 13, 12, 9, 12, 10, 13, 11, 10, 12, x

a If there are two modes, what are the possible values of x?

b If there is exactly one mode, write a possible value for x, and the mode.

10 The table below shows the number of light bulbs that need to be replaced on each floor of a building in a month. The total number of floors in the building is 38.

Number of Replaced Light Bulbs on Each Floor of a Building

Number of Light Bulbs	0	1	2	3	4	5	6	7
Number of Floors	2	5	x	6	8	5	y	3

a The mode for this set of data is 4. The value of x is greater than the value of y. Find the greatest possible value of x and its corresponding value of y.

b Find the median number of light bulbs that need to be replaced. Use the values of x and y in a.

 c Find the mean number of light bulbs that need to be replaced. Use the values of x and y in a. Round your answer to the nearest whole number.

Chapter 13
Extra Practice and Homework
Measure of Central Tendency and Variability

Activity 4 Interpreting Quartiles and Interquartile Range

Find the median, the lower quartile, the upper quartile, and the interquartile range of each data set.

1 Ages of a group of basketball coaches:
24, 44, 16, 37, 28, 29, 52, 58, 32, and 43

2 Monthly average temperature, in °F , in Dallas, Texas:
65, 68, 76, 86, 97, 104, 108, 106, 98, 55, 71, and 66

3 The speed, in kilometer per hour, of ten vehicles:
73, 67, 73, 90, 102, 78, 76, 80, 86, and 100

4 Average height, in feet, of some apple trees:
16, $27\frac{1}{2}$, $19\frac{1}{4}$, 31, 19, $25\frac{1}{2}$, 22, 14, $32\frac{3}{4}$, $27\frac{5}{8}$, 26, and 29

Solve.

5 The table shows the results of 18 students on a 50-point quiz.

34 29 38 46 26 47 40 39 45

30 41 22 28 35 20 18 34 38

a Find the range of the results of the students.

b Find the first quartile, the second quartile, and third quartile of the scores.

c Find the interquartile range.

d Interpret the interquartile range.

6 The table shows the amount of time, in minutes, 15 patients waited to see a doctor.

Time (min)	8	9	10	11	12	13	14	15	16
Number of People	1	1	0	4	2	1	5	0	1

a Find the range of the duration.

b Find the median, first, and third quartiles of the scores.

c Find the interquartile range.

d What percent of the patients waited between 11 and 14 minutes to see the doctors?

7 The brake reaction time of 280 motorists is summarized into quartiles below.

First quartile = 1.2 seconds
Second quartile = 1.8 seconds
Third quartile = 2.7 seconds

a How many motorists have a brake reaction time of less than 2.7 seconds?

b How many motorists have a brake reaction time of more than 1.2 seconds but less than 1.8 seconds?

Chapter 13

Extra Practice and Homework
Measure of Central Tendency and Variability

Activity 5   Box Plots and Mean Absolute Deviation

For each box plot, state the least value, the greatest value, the median, the lower quartile, and the upper quartile. Then, find the interquartile range.

1

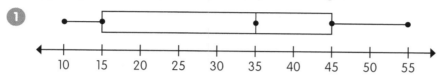

2

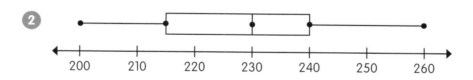

3

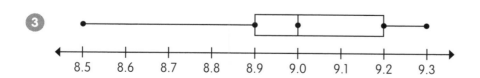

Draw a box plot for each set of the five values.

4 Lower quartile = 40, median = 45, upper quartile = 55, least value = 20, greatest value = 70

5 Lower quartile = 57.5, median = 65.0, upper quartile = 70, least value = 35, greatest value = 75

6 Lower quartile = 825, median = 900, upper quartile = 950, least value = 725, greatest value = 1,000

Calculate the mean absolute deviation for each data set. Round your answer to the nearest hundredth, where necessary.

 173, 197, 200, 155, 150, 134, 125, 169, 141, 241, 225, and 184

8 76, 59, 91, 67, 73, 95, 78, 84, 71, 83, 47, 68, 91, 77, and 80

9 589, 745.6, 491, 921, 567.8, 589, 426.8, 631, 487.6, 468, 495.6, and 835.6

Solve.

10 The typing speed, in words per minute, of 15 typists are as shown.

38	31	23	41	29	27	29	27	33	44
28	29	28	27	31

a Calculate the lower quartile, the median, and the upper quartile.

b Draw a box plot of the typing speeds.

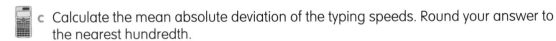 **c** Calculate the mean absolute deviation of the typing speeds. Round your answer to the nearest hundredth.

Chapter 13

Extra Practice and Homework
Measure of Central Tendency and Variability

Activity 6   Real-World Problems: Measures of Central Tendency and Variability

Solve.

1 The amount of honey harvested, in gallons, from a hive for 18 years is 5, 7, 4, 7, 7, 6, 7, 8, 8, 4, 5, 8, 6, 7, 5, 6, 5, and 8. Find the mean, median, and mode. Round your answers to the nearest tenth of a gallon.

2 The table shows the number of windows in 60 houses.

Number of Windows in 60 Houses

Number of Windows	2	3	4	5	6	7	8
Number of Houses	4	4	7	15	16	8	6

a Find the mean, median, and mode.

b Which measure of central tendency best describes the data set? Explain your answer.

3 The data set shows the number of hours 27 students spent online shopping during one week.

0, 0, 0, 0, 1, 1, 1, 1, 2, 2, 2, 2, 2, 2, 2, 2, 3, 3, 3, 3, 3, 3, 2, 2, 2, 1, 1

a Find the mean, median, and mode.

b What is the least whole number you should include in the data set if you want the mean to be greater than the median?

4　The dot plot shows a city's daily low temperature, in degrees Celsius, for 40 days.

Briefly describe the distribution and relate the measure of center to the shape of the dot plot shown.

5 The dot plot shows the number of public holidays in 21 countries. Each dot represents 1 country.

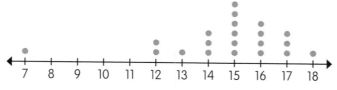

Number of Public Holidays

a Find the mean, median, and mode.

b Give a reason why the mean is less than the median.

c Which measure of central tendency best describes the data set? Explain your answer.

d Relate the measures of center to the shape of the data distribution.

6 The lengths of 23 leaves were correctly measured to the nearest centimeter.

The following information is known about the results.

- The number of leaves that measure 3 centimeters is half the number of leaves measuring 8 centimeters and 9 centimeters. It is also two times the number of leaves measuring 2 centimeters.

- The ratio of the number of leaves measuring 10 centimeters to the number of leaves measuring 11 centimeters to the number of leaves measuring 12 centimeters is 1 : 2 : 1.

- There are 2 more leaves measuring 10 centimeters than leaves measuring 2 centimeters.

a Draw a dot plot to show the data.

b Briefly describe the data distribution and relate the measure of center to the shape of the dot plot shown.

7 The test scores for two classes, A and B, are summarized in the box plots.

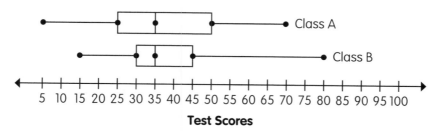

Class A

Class B

5 10 15 20 25 30 35 40 45 50 55 60 65 70 75 80 85 90 95 100

Test Scores

a Compare the medians of the scores for the two classes.

b Compare the interquartile ranges of the scores for the two classes.

c Relate the interquartile ranges to the distributions. Which class has greater variability in the test scores? Explain your answer.

8 The table shows the time to complete the same bus route by Company P and Company Q for a week.

	Time Taken to Complete Bus Route						
Company P	35	23	34	32	34	25	27
Company Q	34	43	41	34	35	36	43

a Find the mean time taken, in minutes, by each company.

b Calculate the mean absolute deviation of the time taken, in minutes, by each company.

c Compare the means and mean absolute deviations of the time taken by the two companies. Which company showed less variability in the time taken to complete the same bus route? Explain your answer.

Mathematical Habit 4 Use mathematical models

Consider the two scenarios below.

a The table shows the number of cell phones owned by 1,000 people in a country.

Number of Cell Phones	0	1	2	3	4	5	6	7	8
Number of People	19	343	285	37	132	83	28	6	67

Explain which measure of central tendency best describes the average number of cell phones each person owned in the country.

b There are 10 employees in a factory. Out of the employees, one of them is the supervisor and the rest are workers. The salary of the supervisor is $5,300 and each of the workers earns $1,700. Explain which measure of central tendency best describes the average salary earned by the employees in the factory.

Mathematical Habit 1 Persevere in solving problems

The number of members in a society in January, March, May, and June of a particular year are 204, 208, 150, and 140 respectively. The mean number of members during the first six months of the year is $184\frac{1}{3}$.

If the number of members in April drops by 25%, the mean number of members becomes $175\frac{2}{3}$. How many members are there in February and April?